Toasts

To Jim Bertagnoli, who in a sense made it all possible.
And to Patti, Matt, Gary and Mary Sue, Bill and Emil, Jerry and Joyce,
Craig and Lenny, Charlie and Mary, Nick and Honey, Ralph and Beth,
Greg and Eileen, Chuck and Sara, Tom and Lee, and all the rest of you.

Here's to ya!

Toasts

The Illustrated Book of
Drinking Poems, Salty
Salutations, Eloquent Epithets
& Vivid Verbosity

WILLOW CREEK PRESS

Minocqua, Wisconsin

© 1994 Willow Creek Press

Photographs courtesy of the Library of Congress.

ISBN 1-57223-012-6

Published by WILLOW CREEK PRESS
            an imprint of Outlook Publishing
            P.O. Box 881
            Minocqua, WI 54548

For information on other Willow Creek titles, write or call 1-800-850-WILD.

Printed in the U.S.A.

Contents

Wine

When Father Time swings round his scythe,
Intomb me 'neath the bounteous vine,
So that its juices red and blithe,
May cheer these thirsty bones of mine.
—Eugene Field

May the joys of today be those of tomorrow,
The goblet of life holds no days of sorrow.
—Foreman.

May the brimming bowl with a wreath be crowned,
    And quaff the draught divine !
Comrades, not in the world is found
    Such another wine.

Grasp the bowl; in nectar sinking
Man of sorrow, drown thy thinking!

❧

Come goblet—nymph, of heavenly shape,
Pour the rich weepings of the grape.

❧

When I drink, the bliss is mine;
There's bliss in every drop of wine!

❧

Now, drop thy goblet's richest tear
In exquisite libation here!

❧

God made man
As frail as a bubble,
God made love,
And love made trouble,
God made wine,
And is it any sin
For man to drink wine
To drown trouble in?

❧

Let schoolmasters puzzle their brain
With grammar and nonsense and learning;
Good liquor, I stoutly maintain,
Gives genius a better discerning.
—Goldsmith.

❧

Here's to a " Dram " and a good long one.

❧

Drink wine! for I tell thee four times o'er and more,
Return there is none!—Once gone we are gone forever!

❧

Yes, be the glorious revel mine,
Where humor sparkles from the wine!

❧

Here is a riddle most abstruse:
Cans't read the answer right?
Why is it that my tongue grows loose
Only when I grow tight?

❧

Press the grape and let it pour
Around the board its purple show'r;
And while the sweet drops our goblets fill,
We'll anticipate the joyous thrill.

❧

Today we'll haste to quaff our wine,
As if tomorrow ne'er should shine;
But if tomorrow comes, why then—
We'll haste to quaff our wine again.

❧

That Adam ate, not that he drank,
Was he from Eden's garden driven;
And what he lost by eating then
To us anew by wine is given;
Yes! wine restores those Eden days,
So here's to wine and jolly lays!

Say, why did Time
His glass sublime
Fill up with sand unsightly,
When wine, he knew,
Runs brisker through
And sparkles far more brightly.

❧

Mix me, now, a cup divine,
Crystal water, ruby wine:
Here—upon this holy bowl,
I surrender all my soul.

❧

Here's to old wine and young
women.

❧

You know, my Friends, with what a brave carouse
I made a second Marriage in my house;
Divorced old barren Reason from my bed,
And took the Daughter of the Vine to spouse.

I pray thee, by the gods above,
Give me the mighty bowl I love,
And let me sing, in wild delight,
"I will—I will be mad tonight!"

When I drink, I feel, I feel,
Visions of poetic zeal!
Warm with the goblets fresh'ning dews,
My heart invokes the heavenly Muse.

While our inglorious, placid souls
Breathe not a wish beyond the bowls,
Fill them from high ye ruddy slaves,
And bathe us in their honied waves!

Why, be this juice the growth of God, who dare
Blaspheme the twisted tendril as a snare?
A blessing, we should us it, should we not?
And if a curse—why, then, who set it there?

Here's to a fresh bumper—for why should we go
While the nectar still reddens our cups as they flow?
Pour out the rich juices still bright with the sun,
Till o'er the brimmed crystal the rubies shall run.
The purple-globed clusters their life-dews have bled;
How sweet is the breath of the fragrance they shed!

Here's to a long life and a merry one,
A quick death and an easy one,
A pretty girl and a true one,
A cold bottle and another one.

❧

In woman I'll take youth, and seek for
    age in wine.

❧

    Here's to the girl I love,
I wish that she were nigh;
    If drinking beer would bring her here,
I'd drink the damn place dry.

❧

I wish that my room had a floor;
I don't so much care for a door,
But this walking around
Without touching the ground
Is getting to be such a bore.
                              —Burgess.

❧

The drink comforteth the brain and
    heart and helpeth the digestion.
                              —Francis Bacon.

❧

Who loves not women, wine and song,
Will be a fool his whole life long.

❧

Friend of my soul! this goblet sip—
   'Twill chase the pensive tear;
'Tis not so sweet as a woman's lip,
   But, O! 'tis more sincere.

∽

'Tween woman and wine a man's lot is to smart,
For wine makes his head ache and woman his heart.

∽

Let us have wine and women, mirth and laughter,
Sermons and soda-water the day after.
            —Lord Byron

∽

For Summer's last roses lie hid in the wines
That were garnered by maidens who laughed
　　through the vines.
Then a smile and a glass and a toast and a cheer,
For all the good wine, and we've some of it here!
In cellar, in pantry, in attic, in hall,
Long live the gay servant that laughs for us all!
　　　　　　　　—Holmes.

Now quickly by the Tavern Door agape,
Came shining through the dusk a nymphean
　　shape
Bearing a vessel on her shoulder; and
She bid me taste of it; and 'twas the grape!

Fill up, fill up and let us swim
Our souls upon the goblet's brim;
Age begins to blanch the brow,
We've time for nought but pleasure
    now.

❧

Before our fading years decline,
Let us quaff the brimming wine.

❧

I'll quaff, my boy, and calmly sink
This soul to slumber as I drink.
Soon, too soon, my comrade brave,
You'll deck your partner's grassy grave;
And there's an end—for ah! you know
They drink but little wine below.

Wine is good, love is good,
And all is good if understood;
The sin is not in doing,
But in overdoing.
How much of mine has gone that way?
Alas! How much more that may?

❧

Some take their gold
In minted mold,
And some in harps hereafter,
But give me mine
In bubbles fine,
And keep the change in laughter.

❧

TO CHAMPAGNE

Here's to champagne, the drink divine,
    That makes us forget our troubles;
It's made of a dollar's worth of wine
    And three dollars' worth of bubbles

A Book of Verses underneath the Bough,
A Jug of Wine a Loaf of Bread—and Thou
Beside me singing in the wilderness—
Oh, Wilderness were Paradise enow!
              —From the Persian

Before our fading years decline,
Let us quaff the brimming wine.

Behold my wine-glass, 'tis filled to the brim,
With soul-stirring nectar, and I drink it to him,
Who feels, as he kisses its contents away,
It was made to gladden, and not to betray,
For wine is like woman, and like her was given
To man on earth as a foretaste of heaven;
Like her eye it sparkles; like her cheek it glows,
When pressed to the lips of the lover who knows
How to keep and cherish these treasures of earth;
For him was woman made, for him the wine's birth;
Then fill up your glasses, fill quite to the brim,
And drink with me to the health of him
Who feels as he kisses its contents away
It was made to gladden, but not to betray.
   Merrily yours,
   Marshal P. Wilder

No churchman am I to rail and to write,
No statesman nor soldier to plot or to fight,
No sly man of business contriving a snare,
For a big-belly'd bottle's the whole of my care.

Within this goblet, rich and deep,
I cradle all my woes to sleep.

A fig then for Burgundy, Claret or Mountain,
A few scanty glasses must limit your wish;
But he's the true toper that goes to the fountain,
The drinker that verily "drinks like a fish!"

" 'A wet night maketh a dry morning,'
Quoth Hendyng, 'rede ye right;
And the cure most fair is the self-same hair
Of the dog that gave the bite.' "
       —Punderson.

Drink and the world drinks with you,
 Swear off and you drink alone.

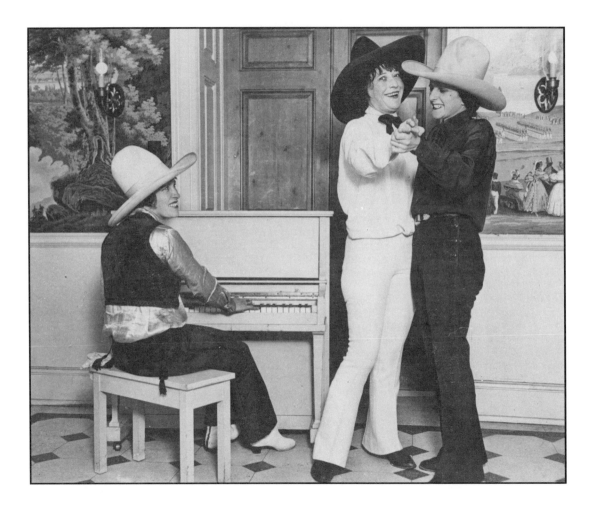

Women

Drink to fair woman, who, I think,
    Is most entitled to it,
For if anything ever can drive me to drink,
    She certainly could do it.
                —B. Jabez Jenkins.

As for the women, though we scorn and flout 'em,
We may live with, but not without them.

May the blossoms of love never be blighted,
And a true-hearted young woman never be slighted.

There's not a place in earth or heaven,
There's not a task to mankind given,
There's not a blessing or a woe,
There's not a whispered yes or no,
There's not a life or birth,
That has a feather's weight of worth—
    without a woman in it.

✧

Health to the bold and dashing coquette,
    Who careth not for me;
Whose heart, untouched by love as yet,
    Is wild and fancy free.

✧

A mocking eye,
A pair of lips
That's often why
A fellow trips.

✧

MY RIVAL

I go to concert, party, ball—
What profit is in these?
I sit alone against the wall
And strive to look at ease.
The incense that is mine by right
They burn before Her shrine;
And that's because I'm seventeen
And She is forty-nine.

I cannot check my girlish blush,
My color comes and goes;
I redden to my fingertips,
And sometimes to my nose.
But She is white where white should be,
And red where red should shine.
The blush that flies at seventeen
Is fixed at forty-nine.

I wish I had Her constant cheek:
I wish that I could sing
All sorts of funny little songs.
Not quite the proper thing.
I'm very gauche and very shy,
Her jokes aren't in my line;
And, worst of all, I'm seventeen
While She is forty-nine.

The young men come, the young men go
Each pink and white and neat,
She's older than their mothers, but
They grovel at Her feet.
They walk beside Her rickshaw wheels—
None ever walk by mine;
And that's because I'm seventeen
And She is forty-nine.

She rides with half a dozen men
(She calls them " boys" and "mashers"),
I trot along the Mall alone;
My prettiest frocks and sashes
Don't help to fill my programme-card,
And vainly I repine
From ten to two A.M. Ah me!
Would I were forty-nine!

She calls me "darling, " "pet," and "dear,"
And "sweet retiring maid."
I'm always at the back, I know,
She puts me in the shade.
She introduces me to men,
"Cast" lovers, I opine,
For sixty takes to seventeen,
Nineteen to forty-nine.

But even She must older grow
And end Her dancing days,
She can't go on forever so
At concerts, balls, and plays.
One ray of priceless hope I see
Before my footsteps shine;
Just think, that She'll be eighty-one
When I am forty-nine.

—Rudyard Kipling

Secrets with girls, like guns with boys,
Are never valued 'till they make a noise.
—Crabbe.

THE DRINKERS PROGRESS.

PUBLISHED BY G. W. EDMONDSON, PLYMOUTH, RICHLAND COUNTY, OHIO.

He is "Cleaned Out."

Love

May those now love
   Who've never loved before,
May those who've loved
   Now love the more.

The night has a thousand eyes,
   And the day but one;
Yet the light of the whole world dies
   With the dying sun;
The mind has a thousand eyes,
   And the heart but one;
Yet the light of a whole life dies
   When love is done.

Here's to Love—the only fire against
   which there is no insurance.

Here's to love, liberty and length of
   blissful days.

No soul can ever clearly see
Another's highest, noblest part;
Save through the sweet philosophy
And loving wisdom of the heart.

Here's a health to the Future;
    A sigh for the Past;
We can love and remember,
    And hope to the last.

Here's to somebody—
Somewhere, somebody
Makes love to somebody,
    Tonight.

Alas, the love of woman! it is know
To be a lovely and a fearful thing.
                    —Byron

Here's to our wives and sweethearts—
And may they never meet.

Here's to our sweethearts and our wives;
May our sweethearts soon become our wives.
And our wives ever remain our sweethearts.

Here's to the prettiest,
Here's to the wittiest,
    Here's to the truest of all who are true,
Here's to the neatest one,
Here's to the sweetest one,
    Here's to them all in one—here's to you.

Here's to the girl that I love,
    And here's to the girl who loves me,
And here's to all that love her whom I love,
    And all those that love her who loves me.

Let's be gay while we may,
    And seize love with laughter.
I'll be true as long as you,
    And not a moment after.

You gave me the key of your heart, my love;
    Then why do you make me knock?
Oh, that was yesterday, Saints above!
    And last night—I changed the lock!
            —John Boyle O'Reilly.

A mighty pain to love it is,
And 'tis a pain that pain to miss;
But of all pains the greatest pain
It is to love and love in vain.

I will drink to the woman who wrought my woe
In the diamond morning of long ago;
To the splendor caught from the orient skies
That thrilled in the dark of her hazel eyes,
Her large eyes filled with the fire of the south,
And the dewy wine of her warm red mouth.
　　　　　　　—Winter.

Here's to the lasses we've loved, my lad,
Here's to the lips we've pressed;
    For of kisses and lasses,
Like liquor in glasses,
    The last is always the best.

May we all be blessed with love from one, friendship
    from many and goodwill from all.

Never look sad, there's nothing so bad
    As getting familiar with sorrow;
Treat him today in a cavalier way,
    And he'll seek other quarters tomorrow.

May her voyage through life be as happy and as free
As the dancing waves on the deep blue sea.

Here's to woman, present and past,
   And those who come hereafter;
But if one comes here after us,
   We'll have no cause for laughter.

Here's to my wife!
Wish her long life!
She's mighty good looking, unrivaled at cooking;
Knows all about medicine, as inventive as Edison;
Just plumb full of grit, has no equal for wit;
Sees the point when I joke, insists that I smoke;
Never chews the rag when I get a jag;
She knows how to sew, still calls me her beau.

Here's to her who halves our sorrows and
    doubles our joys.

⁂

Here's to the wedding ring worn thin;
    ah, summers not a few,
Since I put it on your finger first,
    have passed o'er me and you
And, love, what changes we have seen—
    what cares and pleasures, too—
Since you became my own dear wife,
    when this old ring was new.

⁂

A good wife and health
Are a man's best wealth.

⁂

Come, dear wife, fill the bowl,
I drink to love and thee;
Thou never can'st decay in soul,
Thou'lt still be young to me.

⁂

Here's to the lad valiant and bold,
Who kiss'd the maid modest and meek;
When he'd kiss'd one side times untold
She calmly turned the other cheek.
          —Harry Hawkeye.

⁂

They say microbes dwell in a kiss
This rumor is most rife,
Come, lady dear, and make of me
An invalid for life.

Drink to me only with thine eyes,
And I will pledge with mine;
Or leave a kiss within the cup,
And I'll not look for wine,
The thirst that from the soul doth rise
Doth ask a drink divine:
But might I of Jove's nectar Sup,
I would not change from thine.
                    —Ben Johnson.

May we kiss all the girls we please, and
    please all the girls we kiss.

TO TWO COUPLES

Here's to you two and to we two;
    If you two love we two
As we two love you two,
    Then here's to we four;
But if you two don't love we two,
    As we two love you two,
Then here's to we two and no more.

Were't the last drop in the well,
    As I gasp'd upon the brink,
Ere my fainting spirit fell,
    'Tis to thee that I would drink.
                    —Byron.

Here's to the merry old world,
    And the days—be they bright or blue—
Here's to the Fates, let them bring what they may,
    But the best of them all—That's you!

❧

Here's to you as good as you are,
    And to me as bad as I am;
As good as you are and as bad as I am,
    I'm as good you are, as bad as I am.

❧

Here's to one and only one,
    And may that one be she
Who loves but one and only one,
    And may that one be me.

❧

A cheerful glass, a pretty lass,
    A friend sincere and true,
Blooming health, good store of wealth,
    Attend on me and you.

When e'er with friends I drink
Of one I always think:
She's pretty, she's witty, and so true;
So with joy and great delight
I'll drink to her tonight,
And when doing so think none the less of you!

Marriage

Strohmeyer & Wyman, Publishers,
New York, N.Y.

a could shee yourself th'-way I shee you, you would be 'stonished too."

Here's to marriage, a feast where the grace is some-
    times better than the dinner.

Here's to marriage, an institution where one person
    undertakes to provide happiness for two.

How like this bowl of wine, my fair,
Our loving life shall fleet;
Though tears may sometimes mingle there,
The draught will still be sweet!

Misfortunes never come single,
And so, like birds of feather,
The marriages and the deaths
Are always printed together.

Ah, my Beloved, fill the cup that clears
    Today of past regret and future fears:
Tomorrow!—Why, tomorrow I may be
    Myself with yesterday's seven thousand years.

The Happy Couple—May we all live to be present at
their golden wedding.

&

Let us drink to their health and prosperity; may they
have a joyous bridal trip, and may their journey through
life be over a pleasant road without any embarrassment
that energy and love cannot easily overcome.

&

May the single be married and the married happy.

&

Wedlock's like wine—not properly judged of till the
second glass.
—Jarrold.

Every wedding, says the proverb,
Makes another, soon or late.
Never yet was marriage entered
In the heavenly book of fate.
But what the names were also written,
Of a patient pair who wait.

Whose will be the next occasion
For the flowers, the feast, the wine?
Thine, perchance, fairest maiden,
Or, who knows it may be mine.
What if 'twere, forgive the fancy,
What if 'twere both thine and mine?

Life

COMFORT

SAY! You've struck a heap of trouble—
Bust in business, lost your wife;
No one cares a cent about you,
You don't care a cent for life;
Hard luck has of hope bereft you,
Health is failing, wish you'd die—
Why, you've still the sunshine left you
And the big, blue sky.

Sky so blue it makes you wonder
If it's heaven shining through;
Earth so smiling 'way out yonder,
Sun so bright it dazzles you;
Birds a-singing, flowers a-flinging
All their fragrance on the breeze;
Dancing shadows, green, still meadows—
Don't you mope, you've still got these.
These, and none can take them from you;
These, and none can weigh their worth.

What! you're tired and broke and beaten?—
Why, you're rich—you've got the earth!
Yes, if you're a tramp in tatters,
While the blue sky bends above
You've got nearly all that matters—
You've got God, and God is love.
                        —Robert Service

⁒

THE WORLD'S ALL RIGHT

Just try to get the Cosmic touch,
The sense that you don't matter much.
A million stars are in the sky;
A million planets plunge and die;
A million million men are sped;
A million million wait ahead.
Each plays his part and has his day—
    What ho! the World's all right, I say.

Just try to get the Chemic view:
A million million lives made "you."
In lives a million you will be
Immortal down Eternity;
Immortal on this earth to range,
With never death, but ever change.
You always were, and will be aye—
    What ho! the World's all right, I say.

Be glad! And do not blindly grope
For Truth that lies beyond our scope:
A sober plot informeth all
Of Life's uproarious carnival.
Your day is such a little one,
A gnat that lives from sun to sun;
Yet gnat and you have parts to play—
    What ho! the World's all right, I say.

And though it's written from the start,
Just act your best your little part.
Just be as happy as you can,
And serve your kind, and die—a man.
Just live the good that in you lies,
And seek no guerdon of the skies;
Just make your Heaven here, today—
    What ho! the World's all right, I say.
              —Robert Service

Life's a jest, and all things show it;
I thought so once and now I know it.
                    —Gay.

❧

While we live, let's live in clover,
For when we're dead, we're dead all
    over.

❧

As we ride over the bad roads of life,
    may good wine be our spur.

❧

May the Lord love us. but not
    call us too soon.

❧

After we have weathered the
    storm of life, may we drop
quietly and gratefully into the
    harbor of eternal bliss.

❧

Fill the bowl with flowing wine,
And while your lips are wet,
Press their fragrance into mine
And forget.
Every kiss we take and give
Leaves us less of life to live.

❧

We'll gather Joy's luxuriant flowers,
And gild with bliss our fading hours;
Bacchus shall bid our winter bloom,
And Venus dance us to the tomb!

From out the earth we naked sprang,
Thus to the earth we go;
And since at last we nothing have,
Why should we labor so?

Oh threats of Hell and Hopes of Paradise!
One thing at least is certain—This Life flies;
One thing is certain and the rest is Lies;
The flower that once has blown forever dies.
                    —Omar Khayyám.

Perpetual strife
Is the life
Of mortal man.
In the hot fire
Of pain and desire,
Is unceasingly wrought,
On the forge of thought,
His being's end.
Only at last
Shall the furnace blast,
When he is old,
Grow cold.

May you live as long as you like and
   have all you like as long as you live.

❧

Leave politics to statesmen and thinkers,
But be jolly here with merry drinkers.

❧

The rising sun may kiss the sky,
The morning dew, the butterfly,
The sparkling wine may kiss the glass
And you my friend,
Have a nice day.

❧

There's room in the halls of pleasure
For a long and lordly train;
But one by one we must all file on
Through the narrow aisles of pain.

❧

May every day be happier than the last.

❧

Then catch the moments as they fly,
   And use them as ye ought, man;
Believe me, happiness is shy,
   And comes note aye when sought, man.
               —Burns.

❧

May we always imitate those who are happy and
    never envy them.

I drink it as the Fates ordain it,
    Come, fill it, and have done with rhymes;
Fill up the lonely glass and drain it
    In memory of dear old times.

Ah, make the most of what we yet may spend,
Before we too into the dust descend
Dust into dust and under dust to lie,
Sans wine, sans song, sans singer, and—sans end!
             —From the Persian.

Jack be nimble, Jack be quick,
Jack jumped over the candlestick.
    Great balls of fire!

Ah, fill the cup—what boots it to repeat
How Time is slipping underneath our feet;
Unborn tomorrow, and dead yesterday,
Why fret about them if today be sweet!

The moving finger writes; and having writ,
Moves on: nor all our piety nor wit
Shall lure it back to cancel half a line,
Nor all our tears wash out a word of it.

Enjoy the spring of Love and Youth,
To some good angel leave the rest,
For all too soon we learn the truth;
There are no birds in the last year's nest.

We come into this world all naked and bare;
We go through this world full of sorrow and care;
We go out of this world. we know not where,
But if we're good fellows here, we'll be thoroughbreds
    there.

Friendship

A glass is good, a lass is good,
    And a pipe to smoke in cold weather,
The world is good and the people are good,
    And we're all good fellows together.

Happy the man, and happy he alone,
He who can call today his own;
He who, secure within, can say
Tomorrow, do thy worst, for I have lived today.
                      —Dryden.

A dinner, coffee and cigars,
    Of friends, a half a score,
Each favorite vintage in its turn—
    What man could wish for more?

Happy days.

꙰

Set 'em up again.

꙰

May good humor preside when
    good fellows meet,
And reason prescribe when 'tis
    time to retreat.

꙰

Heaven give thee many, many
    merry days.
             —Shakespeare.

꙰

There's fellowship
In every sip
Of friendship's brew.

Here's to the four hinges of Friendship—
Swearing, Lying, Stealing and Drinking.
When you swear, swear by your country;
When you lie, lie for a pretty woman,
When you steal, steal away from bad company
And when you drink, drink with me.

Let's have a nip.

Here's to you, as good as you are,
Here's to me, as bad as I am.
And as bad as I am, and as good as you are,
You'll never be as good as I am
        As bad as you are.

He who goes to bed, and goes to bed sober,
Falls as the leaves do, and dies in October;
But he who goes to bed, and does so mellow,
Lives as he ought to, and dies a good fellow.
                    —Parody on Fletcher.

⚬

Here's to those who love us,
And here's to those who don't,
A smile for those who are willing to,
And a tear for those who won't.

⚬

To drink tonight, with hearts as light,
To loves as gay and fleeting
As bubbles that swim on the breakers' brim,
And break on the lips while meeting.
                    —Charles Hoffman.

To the old, long life and treasure;
To the young, all health and pleasure.
Let the world slide, let the world go;
A fig for care, and a fig for woe;
If I can't pay, why I can owe,
And death makes equal the high and low.
                                                —Heywood.

❧

Comrades, pour the wine tonight,
For the parting is with dawn.
Oh! the clink of cups together,
With the daylight coming on!
Greet the morn
With a double horn,
When strong men drink together.
                                        —Richard Hovey.

❧

In for a high old frolic,
Chiefly alcoholic.

❧

Care to our coffins adds a nail, no doubt;
And every grin so merry draws one out.
                                        —Dr. Wolcot.

❧

Here's to mine and here's to thine!
Now's the time to clink it!
Here's a flagon of old wine,
And here we are to drink it.
                                        —Richard Hovey.

❧

THE MADNESS OF PRIVATE ORTHERIS

Oh! Where would I be when my froat was dry?
Oh! Where would I be when the bullets fly?
Oh! Where would I be when I come to die?
Why,
    Somewheres anigh my chum.
    If 'e's liquor 'e'll give me some,
    If I'm dyin' 'e'll 'old my 'ead,
    An' 'e'll write 'em 'ome when I'm dead—
    Gawd send us a trusty chum!
                —Barrack-Room Ballad, from
                the *Works of Rudyard Kipling*

Happy are we met, happy have we been,
Happy may we part, and happy meet again.

Had Neptune when first he took charge of the Sea,
Been as wise, or at least been as merry as we,
He'd have thought better on't and instead of his brine,
Would have filled the vast ocean with generous wine.
                    —Mr. Popely.

❧

Come, once more, a bumper!—then drink as you please,
Tho' who could fill halfway to toasts such as these?
Here's our next joyous meeting—and, oh, when we meet,
May our wine be as bright and our union as sweet!
                    —Tom Moore.

❧

Drink, boys, drink, and drive away sorrow—
Perhaps we may not drink again tomorrow.

❧

Some men want youth and others health,
Some from a wife will often shrink;
Some men want wit and others wealth—
May we want nothing but to drink.

The melancholy days are come, the saddest of the year;
Not cold enough for whiskey hot, but too damn cold for beer.

Thus circling the cup, hand in hand, ere we drink,
    Let sympathy pledge us, through pleasure, through pain,
That, fast as feeling but touches one link,
    Her magic shall send it direct through the chain.

Be rich and the men will seek you,
    Poor, and they turn and go—
You're a mighty good fellow when you are mellow,
    And your pockets are lined with dough.
Be flush and your friends are many,
    Go broke and you lose them all.
You're a dandy old sport at $4.00 a quart,
    But not if you chance to fall.

Friendly may we part and quickly meet again.

Here's hoping that My Uncle's Niece,
And your Aunt's Nephew
May always be the best of friends.

Here's to the hand of friendship,
Sincere, twice-tried and true.
That smiles in the hour of triumph
And laughs at its joy with you,
Yet stands in the night of sorrow
Close by when the shadows fall,
And never turns the picture
Of an old friend to the wall.

❧

Long be the flame of memory found,
Alive within the social glass,
Let that be still the magic round,
O'er which oblivion dares not pass!

❧

May we be rich in friends rather than
    money.

Among the good things
    That good wine brings,
What is better than laughter,
    That rings
In a revery,
    That makes better friends
Of you and me.

❧

Here's to the friends we class as old,
    And here's to those we class as new;
May the new soon grow to us old,
    And the old ne'er grow to us new.

❧

Fill up the lonely glass, and drain it
In memory of dear old times.

Friendship above all ties bind the heart
And faith in friendship is the noblest part.
                    —Earl of Owery.

At all your feasts, remember too,
When cups are sparkling to the brim
That there is one who drinks to you,
And oh! as warmly drink to him.

Distress not with thy troubles other souls,
Since life has thorns enough for all;
With kind and tender heart and helpful hand,
Gain strength by lifting those who fall.

I've set my heart upon nothing, you see;
    Hurrah!
And so the world goes well with me,
    Hurrah!
And who has a mind to be a fellow of mine,
Why, let him take hold and help me drain
    This loving cup of wine.

The Lord gives our relatives,
Thank God we can choose our friends.

Here's to the triple alliance—
Friendship, Freedom and Wine.

Here's Champagne to our real friends.
And real pain to our sham friends.

Wash me when dead in the juice of the wine, dear friends!
Let your funeral service be drinking and wine, dear friends!
And if you would meet me again when the Doomsday comes,
Search the dust of the tavern, and sift from it mine, dear friends!

TO OUR ABSENT FRIENDS

Although out of sight, we recognize them with our glasses.

To our Fat Friends: May their shadows never grow less.

The man who has a thousand friends,
Has not a friend to spare,
But he who has one enemy,
Will meet him everywhere."

May we treat our friends with kindness and our ene-
mies with generosity.

TO OUR HOST AND HOSTESS

Here's a toast to the host who carved the roast;
And a toast to the hostess—may none ever "roast" us

Here's a health to thee and thine
From the hearts of me and mine;
And when thee and thine
Come to see me and mine,
May me and mine make thee and thine
As welcome as thee and thine
Have ever made me and mine.

I thank you for your welcome which
    was cordial,
And your cordial, which is welcome.

I know thou lov'st a brimming measure,
And art a kindly, cordial host;
But let me fill and drink at pleasure,
Thus I enjoy the goblet most.

May the juice of the grape enliven each soul,
And good humor preside at the head of each bowl.

THE DRINKERS PROGRESS.

Copyright Secured.

Published by G. W. Edmondson, Plymouth, Richland County, Ohio.

12   First Intoxication—Bachelor's Carouse.

Men

"Man wants but little here below,
Nor wants that little long,"
'Tis not with me exactly so;
But 'tis so in the song.
My wants are many, and if told,
Would muster many a score;
And were each wish a mint of gold,
I still should long for more.

What first I want is daily bread—
And canvasbacks—and wine—
And all the realms of nature spread
Before me, when I dine.

Four courses scarcely can provide
My appetite to quell;
With four choice cooks from France beside,
To dress my dinner well.

Here's to the men! God bless them!
Worst of me sins, I confess them!
In loving them all; be they great or small,
So here's to the boys! God bless them!
                    —Grace George's toast
                    in "Pretty Peggy."

❧

Here's to an honest man—The noblest
    work of God.
                    —Andrew Jackson.

❧

The first duty of bachelors—
To ring the city belles.

❧

May all single men be married,
And all married men be happy.

Here's to the man so awf'ly thin,
Who turns somersaults in a sausage skin,
Who casts a shadow that can't be seen.
And coils up like a snake in a soup tureen.
                    —Harry Hawkeye.

Here's to the sincere man!
He makes no friend, who never makes foes.

Ingersoll View Company
St. Paul, Minn U.S.A.
COPYRIGHTED BY
T. W. INGERSOLL, ST. PAUL-1902

..375. "Must 'av had Smashing Good Time."

States & Nations

The Frenchman loves his native wine,
The German loves his beer,
The Englishman loves his 'alf and 'alf,
Because it brings good cheer;
The Irishman loves his "whisky straight,"
Because it gives him dizziness;
The American has no choice at all,
So he drinks the whole damn business.

OLD KAINTUCK

Whar the ladies are beautiful, and whar the crap
    of cawn is utilized for Bourbon.
                        —Eugene Field.

Kentucky, Oh Kentucky! I love thy classic shades,
Where flit the fairy figures of dark-eyed Southern
    maids,
Where the mocking birds are singing 'mid the
    flowers newly born,
Where the corn is full of kernels,
And the colonels full of corn.

VERMONT

What State can beat her in men, women, maple-
    sugar and horses?
"The first are strong, the last are fleet,
 The second and third are exceedingly sweet,
 And all are uncommonly hard to beat."

OLE VIRGINNY

Whar blooms the furtive possum,—pride an' glory of the South!
And anty makes a hoe-cake, sah, that melts within yo mouth.
　　　　　　　　—Eugene Field.

NEW ENGLAND

Where Hubbard squash 'nd huckleberries grow to powerful size,
And everything is orthodox from preachers down to pies.
　　　　　　　　—Eugene Field.

THE WILD AND WOOLLY WEST

Give me no home 'neath the pale pink dome of European skies,
No cot for me by the salmon sea that far to the southward lies;
But away out West I would build my nest on top of a carmine hill,
Where I could paint, without restraint, creation redder still.
        —Eugene Field.

May good fortune follow you all your days,
(And never catch up with you).
        —An Irishman's Toast.

If we do not succeed, Old Ireland to free,
May England hang us on a gooseberry tree.
                    —Odin Optic.

Ireland and America—May the former soon be as free
as the latter, and may the latter never forget that Irishmen
were instrumental in securing the liberty they now enjoy.

THE IRISH EXILE'S TOAST.

Then remember wherever our goblet is crown'd
Thro' this world, whether eastward or westward we roam,
When a cup to the smile of dear woman goes round,
Oh! remember the smile which adorns her at home.

Here's to the land of the shamrock so green,
Here's to each lad and his darling colleen,
Here's to the ones we love dearest and most—
And may God save old Ireland!
    That's an Irishman's toast.

May your soul be in glory three weeks before the divil
    knows you're dead.

SCOTLAND

And lives that man, with soul so dead
Who never to himself hath said—
This is my own, my native land!
                    —Sir Walter Scott.

Wherever I wander, wherever I rove,
The hills of the Highlands forever I love.
                                    —Robt. Burns.

Here's to Scotland! stern and wild,
Meet nurse for a poetic child!
Land of brown heath and shaggy wood,
Land of the mountain and the flood,
Land of my sires! what mortal hand
Can e'er untie the filial band?

Stand to your glasses steady,
    And drink to your comrades' eyes:
Here's a cup to the dead already,
    And hurrah for the next that dies.

ENGLISH

He is an Englishman!
For he himself hath said it,
And it's greatly to his credit,
That he is an Englishman!
For he might have been a Roosian,
A French, or Turk, or Proosian,
Or perhaps Italian?
But in spite of all temptations,
To belong to other nations,
He remains an Englishman.
                                    —W. S. Gilbert.

AN ENGLISHMAN'S TOAST

Daddy Neptune, one day, to Freedom did say,
If ever I lived upon dry land,
The spot I would hit on would be little Britain!
Says Freedom, "Why that's my own island!"
O, it's a snug little island!
A right little, tight little island!
Search the world round, none can be found
So happy as this little island.

TO MEN WITHOUT A COUNTRY

May those who are discontented with their own
   country
leave their country for their country's good.

JAPANESE TOAST TO THE THING WE WANT

Sashi noboru
Asahi no gotoku
Sawayaka ni
Motamahoshiki wa
Kokoro narikeri.

(Translation:)
The thing we want
Is hearts that rise above Earth's
Worries like
The Sun at morn, rising above the clouds,
Splendid and strong.

Wisdom

May we have the unspeakable good fortune to win a
     true heart, and the merit to keep it.

❦

Count that day lost whose low descending sun
Sees at thy hand no worthy action done.

❦

May our pleasures be free from the stings of remorse.

❦

May our talents never be prostituted to vice.

❦

May our wants be sown in so fruitful a soil as to produce immediate relief.

❧

May we never speak to deceive or listen to betray.

❧

Riches without pride or poverty without meanness.

❧

May he who thinks to cheat another, cheat himself most.

❧

May we never murmur without cause, and never have cause to murmur.

❦

May we never be blind to our own errors.

❦

May meanness never accompany riches.

❦

Here's to the Good Things of this World—Parsons are preaching for
them, Lawyers are pleading for them, Physicians are prescribing for
them, Authors are writing for them, Soldiers are fighting for them,
but true Philosophers alone are enjoying them.

❦

Men are born with two eyes, but with one tongue, in
    order that they should see twice as much as they speak.
                —Colton.

&

May the sunshine of comfort dispel the clouds of despair.

&

When two men quarrel, each with tongue aflame,
Who hath the cooler head is most to blame.

&

May we live happy and die in peace with all mankind.

&

May we never flatter our superiors or insult our inferiors.

❧

May he who never wants feeling, never feel want.

❧

May poverty always be a day's march behind us.

❧

May we fly from the temptation we cannot resist.

❧

May genius and merit never want a friend.

∽

May we never be the slaves of interest or pride.

∽

May we always be wise enough to follow the wiser.

∽

May we always do good when we can—
    speak well of the world,
    and never judge without the fullest proof.

∽

May we always think what we would say rather
than say what we think.

❧

May we never let our tongues cut our throats nor
quarrel with our bread and butter.

❧

May we live to learn well
And learn to live well.

❧

May avarice lose his purse and benevolence find it.

❧

When going up the hill of Prosperity,
May you never meet any friend coming down.

Here's to Philosophy—It may conquer past or
    future pain, but toothache, while it lasts, laughs
    at Philosophy.

May we be slaves to no party and bigots to no sect.

May those that are single get wives to their mind,
And those that are married true happiness find.

May the tide of fortune float us into the harbor of content.

❧

May the sword of justice be swayed by the hand of mercy.

❧

May the pole-star of hope guide us through the sea of misfortune.

❧

Power will intoxicate the best hearts, as wine the best heads.

❧

Honest men to law will never go;
Conscience is the only court they know.

❧

May the eye that drops a tear for the misfortunes of others
   never shed one for its own

❧

May virtue be our armor when wickedness is our assailant.

❧

Here's to Charity. the brightest gem in the diadem of
   humanity. It elevates and ennobles those who practise
   and follow its sublime mission in dispelling sorrow and
   suffering. May the luster of its brilliancy never grow dim.

❧

There's not a drop that from our cups we throw
For Earth to drink of, but doth steal below,
To quench the thirst of some imprison'd spirit,
There hidden—far beneath, and long ago.

Speak no word thy secret heart denies;
With his tongue he slays his soul who lies.

Through this toilsome world, alas,
Once, and only once, we pass,
If a kindness we may show,
If a good deed we may do
To our suffering fellow men,
Let us do it when we can,
Nor delay it, for 'tis plain
We shall not pass this way again.

It is easy enough to be pleasant
When life flows along like a song:
But the man worth while is the one who will smile
When everything goes dead wrong.

⁂

May we be rich in friends rather than in money.

⁂

Here's to the other side of the road—it always looks the
cleanest.

⁂

May the pleasures of youth never bring us pain in old age.

So wisely has the Lord God framed these human souls of ours,
That each likes best the place where he doth dwell;
Ask the lost spirits where Perdition is, they'll say in Heaven;
Ask saints, they'll tell you 'tis in Hell.

If solid happiness we prize,
Within our breast this jewel lies,
And they are fools who roam;
The world hath nothing to bestow—
From our own selves our bliss must flow,
And that dear hut, our home.

Home—The place where you are treated best and grumble most.

May we see our own faults rather
than exploit those of our
neighbor.

May our faults be written on the
seashore, and every good action
prove a wave to wash them out.

TO THE GOOD

The good die young—
Here's hoping that you may live to
a ripe old age.

TO THE WORLD

The world's a book writ by th' eternal art
Of the great author; printed in man's heart
'Tis falsely printed, though divinely penned;
And all the errata will appear at th' end.

TO THE WIDOW

Be to her virtues very kind
Be to her faults a little blind.
            —Prior.

Universal Toasts

THE UNIVERSAL TOAST

Observe, when Mother Earth is dry,
She drinks the droppings of the sky,
And then the dewy cordial gives
To every thirsty plant that lives.
The vapors which at evening weep,
Are beverage to the swelling deep;
And when the rosy sun appears,
He drinks the ocean's misty tears.
The moon too quaffs her paly stream
Of lustre from the solar beam.
Then hence with all your sober thinking!
Since Nature's holy law is drinking,
I'll make the law of Nature mine,
And pledge the Universe in wine.

> —Anacreon (Moore's
> translation).

Here's to us all—God bless us every one.
                —Dickens.

I wish thee health,
I wish thee wealth,
I wish thee gold in store,
I wish thee heaven upon earth—
What could I wish thee more?

Here's to us that are here, to you that are
    there, and the rest of us everywhere.
                —Kipling.

May you all be Hung, Drawn and Quartered!
Yes—hung with diamonds,
Drawn in a coach and four,
And quartered in the best houses in the land.

❧

Here's to those that I love;
Here's to those who love me;
Here's to those who love those I love,
And here's to those who love those who love me.
                    —Favorite Toast of Ouida.

❧

The world is filled with flowers,
    The flowers are filled with dew,
The dew is filled with love
    For you and you and you.

Here's to those,
Who wish us well.
Those who don't,
Can go to hell.

❧

Through the lips,
Past the gums,
Look out liver,
Here it comes.

❧

Give it a good home.

❧

TO R-E-M-O-R-S-E.

Those dry Martinis were too much for me,
Last night I really felt immense,
today I feel like thirty cents;
It is no time for mirth and laughter
In the cold gray dawn of the morning after.
                    —George Ade.

⚬

TOAST TO JOHN BARLEYCORN

John Barleycorn was a hero bold,
    Of noble enterprise;
For if you do but taste his blood,
    'Twill make your courage rise.

The saddest words ever composed,
are these dismal four:
    "The bar is closed."

⚬

I have two words for you,
And they're not "Merry Christmas."
                    —Gary Ruschmeyer

⚬

How long was I out?
                    —Craig Tomich

⚬

Wherever you go,
There you are.

You're not an alcoholic if you know some-
one who drinks more than you.
—Lenny Lafredo

TO THE LEGAL FRATERNITY.

Here's to the bride and mother-in-law.
Here's to the groom and father-in-law.
Here's to the sister and brother-in-law.
Here's to the friends and friends-in-law,
May none of them need an attorney-at-law.

TO THE SPENDER

May they never want who have the spirit to
spend.

THE GROCER'S TOAST

May we spring up like vegetables, have turnip-noses,
  reddish cheeks, and carroty hair, and may our
  hearts never be hard, like those of cabbages, nor
  may we be rotten at the core.

THE BLACKSMITH'S TOAST

Success to forgery.

THE BAKER'S TOAST

May we never be done so much as to make us crusty.

Here's to the queen who pounds the keys,
    Who makes you often forget your wife.
With smiling face tries hard to please;
    She's the one bright spot in the office life.

TO THE MEDICAL MAN

Here's to the doctor whose mistakes may be found
All nicely tucked away under the ground.
                            —Odin Optic.

TO A SPORTSMAN

May strength the sportsman's nerves in vigor brace,
And cruelty ne'er stain with fowl disgrace
    The well-earned pleasures of the chase.

TO THE COLLEGE BOY.

Here's to the College Boy!
With his funny clothes and hideous yells;
Who studies football tricks and footlight belles;
Who always is foolish but never bad,
Who spends all the money earned by his dad
He's the village pride and his mother's joy,
So here's long life to the College Boy.

Here's hoping you may always have good health,
    A cosy home and a loving wife;
And the necessary coin in your pocket
    To procure these luxuries of life.

May your feet always go where you want them to;
May your blinking eyes never see double;
May your keyhole stand still in its rightful place,
And the good Lord keep you out of trouble
    When you're drunk.

TOAST TO THE FARMER

Princes and lords may flourish or may fade,
A breath may make them, as a breath has made;
But a bold peasantry, their country's pride,
When once destroyed can never be supplied.

TO POKER

Here's to Poker—Like a glass of beer, you draw to fill.

Here's to you,
  So kind and good.
God must have made you,
  And I wish I could.

Here's to the girl
  Who lives on the hill;
Her daughter won't,
  But her sister will.

WHAT CARE I

I build my castles in the air,
They end in smoke—I don't care.

May the devil never pay visits abroad
  nor receive company at home.

TWO FACED

May the man never grow fat
Who carries two faces under one hat.

TO PARADISE.

Here's to turkey when you are hungry
  Champagne when you are dry,
A pretty girl when you need her
  And heaven when you die.

Here's to the majestic oak, hoary with his centuries—
every oak must be an acorn and great minds
    germinate in cradles.
               —Paul Lowe.

TO THE DEVIL

From his brimstone bed at break of day
A walking the Devil has gone,
To visit his little snug farm of the earth
And see how his stock went on.
Over the hill and over the dale,
And he went over the plain,
And backward and forward he swished his long tail
As a gentleman swishes his cane.

TO GLADNESS, SADNESS, MADNESS

Here's to the gladness of her gladness when she's glad,
Here's to the sadness of her sadness when she's sad;
But the gladness of her gladness,
And the sadness of her sadness,
Are not in it with the madness of her madness when she's mad!

TO THE MEMORY OF GEORGE WASHINGTON

The childless father of ninety millions.

TO ABRAHAM LINCOLN

May eternal life be the portion of him who struck the shackles
from the slaves.

TO DINING

We may live without poetry, music and art,
We may live without conscience and live without heart;
We may live without friends and live without books;
But civilized man cannot live without cooks.
We may live without books—what is knowledge but grieving?
We may live without hope—what is hope but deceiving?
We may live without love—what is passion but pining!
But where is the man that can live without dining?

TO A BAD SINGER

Swans sing before they die; 'twere no bad thing
Did certain persons die before they sing.

TO A SHREW

After such years of dissension and strife,
It's a wonder a man should weep for his wife:
Still his tears on her grave are nothing surprising—
He's laying her dust, for fear of its rising.

TO THE SPRING

Come fill the cup and in the fire of Spring
Your Winter garment of repentance fling:
The Bird of Time has but a little way
To flutter—and the Bird is on the Wing.

TO XMAS

Here's to Christmas, the season which requires Fowl murder to promote
    peace and good will.

TO THANKSGIVING DAY

Here's to the day when first the Yankees
Acknowledged Heaven's good gifts with Thank'ees.

TO WINTER

When it freezes and blows, take care of your nose, that it don't get froze,
    and wrap up your toes in warm woolen hose.

TO A TEAR

When friendship and love our sympathies move,
When Truth in a glance should appear,
The lips may beguile with dimple or smile,
But the test of affection's a tear.

TO AN AFFINITY

Here's to you in wine,
    Good old wine!
I will be your love
    And you will be mine.
I will be constant,
    You will be true,
And I'll leave my happy home and everything
        for you—
    Just for a little while.

OLD SHOES

How much a man is like old shoes,
For instance, both a soul can lose,
Both have been tanned, both are made tight
By cobblers, both get left and right.
Both need a mate to be complete,
And both were made to go on feet.
With shoes the last is first; with man
The first shall be the last; and when
The shoes wear out, they're mended too—
When men wear out they're men dead, too.
They both need heeling, both re-soled,
And both in time turn all to mould,
They both are trod upon, and both
Will tread on others, nothing loath
Both have their ties. and both incline,
When polished, on the world to shine.
They both peg out, so would you choose
To be a man or be his shoes?

SOCIETY

Society is now one polished horde,
Formed of two mighty tribes—
   The bores and bored.

TO OUR BED

In bed we laugh, in bed we cry;
And born in bed, in bed we die:
The near approach the bed may show
Of human bliss to human woe.

TO THE CHILDREN

The world is saved from friend and foe
By what the little children know.

TOAST TO OUR BODIES

When the Supreme our bodies made of clay,
He well foreknew the part that we should play:
Not without his ordainment have we sinned!
Why would he then us burn at judgment day?

TOAST TO NOWHERE

Unworthy of Hell, unfit for Heaven, I be—
God knows what clay He used when me moulded me!
Foul as a punk, ungodly as a monk,
No faith no world, no hope of Heaven I see!

TO SERENITY

Waste not your hour, nor in the vain pursuit
Of this and that endeavor and dispute;
Better be jocund with the fruitful grape
Than sadder after none, or bitter, Fruit.

TO GENEROSITY

He only is generous,
Whose gift,
By willing hand proffered,
Is swift.

TOAST TO A FLOWER

As now the Tulip for her morning sup
Of Heav'nly vintage from the soil looks up
Do you devoutly do the like till Heav'n
To Earth invert you—like an empty cup.

TO THE SUNRISE

Behold the morning! Rise, O youth,
And fill thyself with rosy wine:
From the crystal cup of dawn.
Drink the glowing draught divine!
        —Omar Khayyám

TO ALIMONY

Oh, strenuous days for Cupid,
And Hymen's all astir,
A chap pays court to some fair lass;
The next we hear that comes to pass—
The Court is paying her.

TOAST TO THE ILLS OF LIFE

For every ill beneath the sun
There is some remedy, or none.
Should there be one, resolve to find it;
If not, submit, and never mind it.

TOAST TO BLACK EYES

Here's to the eyes—as black as jet—
Of a charming maid I knew;
I kissed her and her lover came,
And mine were jet-black, too.

Here's to you, my dear,
And to the dear that's not here, my dear,
But if the dear that's not here, my dear,
Were here, my dear,
I'd not be drinking to you, my dear.

TOAST TO VICTORY

Turn failure into victory,
Don't let your courage fade:
And if you get a lemon.
Just make the lemon aid.

TO RICHES

May we never be in possession of
    riches which we cannot enjoy.

May we never be cured of the
    drink habit by lack of pride.

TOAST TO THE MOON

Before thee, Luna, doth I kneel,
Thy radiance to beg;
Come closer to me, orb of night,
And let me pull thy leg.

TOAST TO WIRELESS TELEGRAPHY

A little bird sat on a telegraph wire
And said to his mate, "I declare,
If wireless telegraphy comes into vogue
We'll all have to sit on the air."

TO OUR RICH RELATIONS

Here's to our rich relations!—when we want nothing,
we can always go to them and get it.
                        —Odin Optic.

TO A LANDLADY

Corned beef fresh, and corned beef old,
Corned beef hot, and corned beef cold,
Corned beef tender, and corned beef tough,
Don't you think we have had enough?
　　　　　　　—Harry Hawkeye.

❧

TOAST TO A DOG

O the pup, the beautiful pup,
Drinking his milk from a beautiful cup;
Gambling around so frisky and free,
First gnawing a bone, then biting a flea;
Jumping, running, after the pony;
Beautiful pup, you'll soon be Bologna.

❧

TO MY DOG

Here's to the one that loves me best!
Who shares with me my humble lot,
Who's glad when I am glad
And sorry when I am not;
Who goes wherever I want to go
And never asks me why;
Who does whatever I want him to,
And never told a lie!
　My dog.

❧

TO THE FAITHFUL DOG

Here's to the dog,
That stays at home
And guards the family night and day.
Here's to the dog
That doesn't roam;
But lies on the porch and chases the stray—
The tramp, the burglar, the hen away.
Doesn't a dog's true heart for the household beat,
At morning and evening, in cold and heat?
But he's only a dog!

TOAST TO A BORE

Again I hear that creeking step—
He's rapping at the door!
Too well I know the boding sound
That ushers in a bore.

I do not tremble when I meet
The stoutest of my foes,
But Heaven defend me from the man
Who comes, but never goes.

TO A BABY

O beautiful little baby mine,
I pray you, drink this cordial wine!
It is a wine of virtuous powers;
My mother made it of wild flowers.

TO THE NEW BABY

"The stork has brought a little peach!"
    The nurse said with an air.
"I'm mighty glad," the father said,
    "He didn't bring a pair."

TO A BABY

A lovely being scarcely formed or moulded
A rose with all its sweetest leaves yet folded.
—Byron.

✀

TO BABIES

We haven't all had the good fortune to be
ladies; we have not all been generals, or
poets or statesmen; but when the toast
works down to the babies, we stand on
common ground—for we've all been
babies.

—Mark Twain

✀

TO THE EARTH WE INHABIT

If this little world tonight
Suddenly should fall through space
In a hissing, headlong flight,
Shrivelling from off its face,
As it falls into the sun,
In an instant every trace
Of the little crawling things—
Ants, philosophers, and lice,
Cattle, cockroaches and kings,
Beggars, millionaires and mice,
Men and maggots—all as one
As it falls into the sun—
Who can say but at the same
Instant from some planet far
A child may watch us and exclaim:
"See the pretty shooting star!"
—Herford.

✀

TOAST TO MOTHER

Let others boast of charms divine,
The agile step and graceful air;
More lively is thy wrinkled face,
And threads of silver in thy hair.
I'd rather fold thee in my arms
Than press the sweetest maid that lives;
Thy winter brings more warmth of love
Than all her youthful summer gives.

TO A HAND SQUEEZE

Oh, give me a sly flirtation
By the light of a chandelier—
With music to play in the pauses,
And nobody very near;
Or a seat on a silken sofa,
With a glass of pure old wine,
And mamma too blind to discover
The small white hand in mine.

TO TIMIDITY

Here's to those that love us,
    If we only cared;
Here's to those that we'd love,
    If we only dared.

TO OUR MOTHERS

Now, boys, just a moment! You all had your say,
While enjoying yourselves in so pleasant a way.
We've toasted our sweethearts, our friends and our wives,
We've toasted each other, wishing all merry lives;

But I now will propose to you the toast that is best—
'Tis one in a million, and outshines the rest—
Don't frown when I tell you this toast beats all others—
But drink one more toast, boys, a toast to Our Mothers.

THE SUMMER GIRL

Here's to the heights of Heaven,
Here's to the depths of Hell,
Here's to the girl who can have a good time
And has sense enough not to tell.

Under the turf where the daisies grew
They planted John and his sister Sue,
And their little souls to the angels flew,—
 Boo 'hoo!

What of that peach of the emerald hue,
Warmed by the sun and wet by the dew?
Ah, well, its mission on earth is through.
 Adieu!

TO A WISH

How many sick ones
Wish they were healthy;
How many beggar men
Wish they were wealthy;
How many ugly ones
Wish they were pretty;
How many stupid ones
Wish they were witty;
How many bachelors
Wish they were married;
How many benedicts
Wish they had tarried.
Single or double,
Life's full of trouble;
Riches are stubble,
Pleasure's a bubble.

TOAST TO A PEACH

A little peach in an orchard grew,
A little peach of emerald hue;
Warmed by the sun and wet by the dew,
    It grew.

One day, passing that orchard through,
That little peach dawned on the view
Of Johnny Jones and his sister Sue,
    Them two.

Up at that peach a club they threw,
Down from the stem on which it grew
Fell that peach of emerald hue.
    Mon Dieu!

John took a bite and Sue a chew,
And then the trouble began to brew,
Trouble the doctor couldn't subdue.
    Too true!

TO REGRET

Here's to war—war is hell—my wife's
    first husband was killed at Santiago.

❧

TO SCORN

May fools our scorn, not envy, raise,
For envy is a kind of praise.

❧

TO MODESTY

Here's to modesty, beauty's best
    companion.

❧

TO CARE

A little health, a little wealth,
    A little house and freedom,
With some few friends for certain ends,
    But little cause to need 'em.
And the night shall be filled with music,
    And the cares that infest the day
Shall fold their tents like the Arabs,
    And as silently steal away.
                —Longfellow.

TO GOOD LUCK

Good luck till we are tired of it.

TO THORNS AND FLOWERS

May the thorns of life only serve to
    give a zest to its flowers.

TO LAUGHTER

Laugh at all things,
    Great and small things,
Sick or well, at sea or shore;
    While we're quaffing.
    Let's have laughing.
Who the devil cares for more?
                —Byron.

TO HOPE AND WISHES

Success to our hopes and enjoyment to our wishes.

❧

TO RICHES AND POWER

Riches to the generous and power to the merciful.

❧

TO TEMPTATION AND VIRTUE

May temptation never conquer virtue.

❧

Among the things
That good wine brings,
What is better than laughter,
   That rings
In revelry,
   That makes better friends
   Of you and me?

TO PATIENCE

Here's to the maid who sits
   down to wait for a husband.
Here's to the wife who sits up
   to wait for one.

O trust me, it is no mere fiction, the
   holy fountain of youth;
In the sweet song of the poet it floweth
   in beauty and truth.
         —Schiller.

True wit is nature to advantage dress'd.
What oft was thought, but ne'er so well
   expressed.
         —Pope.

TO PLEASURE
Pleasure that comes unlooked for is
   thrice welcome.

TOAST TO KINDNESS

Have you had a kindness shown?
    Pass it on.
'Twas not given for you alone—
    Pass it on.
Let it travel down the years,
Let it wipe another's tears,
'Till in heaven the deed appears—
    Pass it on.

TO CHEERFULNESS

Cheer up!
What if the day's cold
And you're feeling old
And blue,
And disgusted too?
We all do!
Take a brace,
Look trouble in the face
And smile
Awhile.
Nothing's gained by looking glum—
Keep mum.
Put your woes on the shelf,
Keep your troubles to yourself
And—CHEER UP!

TO BRAVERY

Be strong!
Say not the days are evil—who's to blame?—
And fold the hands and acquiesce. Oh, shame!
Stand up, speak out, and bravely, just the same.

Be strong!
It matters not how deep intrenched the wrong,
How hard the battle goes, the day how long.
Faint not, fight on! tomorrow comes the song.

TO YOUTH

May the youth of our country ever walk in the
   paths of virtue, honor, and truth.

TO MIRTH

Be always as merry as ever you can
For no one delights in a sorrowful man.

"Mirth is the medicine of life,
It cures its ills, it calms its strife;
It softly soothes the brow of care,
And writes a thousand graces there."

ELK'S ELEVEN O'CLOCK TOAST

Look at the clock 'tis the hour of eleven,
Think of those on earth and those in heaven,
Think of wives, sweethearts and mothers,
Drink in silence to our absent brothers.

Here's to those who wish us well,
And those who don't may go to—heaven.

TO A LIE

An abomination unto the Lord, and a
   very potent help in time of trouble.

TO LYING

I do confess, in many a sigh
My lips have breath'd you many a lie,
And who, with such delights in view,
Would lose them for a lie or two?

TO DAME FORTUNE

May Dame Fortune ever smile on you.
But never her daughter—
   Miss Fortune.

'Tis well for some that fortune is
   blind-folded, as many are unworthy
   of her favors.

May fortune recover her eyesight and
   be just in the distribution of her
   favors.

TO FATE

When Fate, at her foot, a broken wreck shall fling me,
And when Fate's hand, a poor plucked fowl shall wring me;
Beware of my Clay, aught else than a bowl to make,
That the scent of the wine new life in time may bring me!

TO HEALTH AND GOOD HUMOR

Give me the nymph who no beauty can boast,
But health and good humor to make me my toast.

To each and all a fair goodnight,
And pleasing dreams and slumbers bright.
— Sir Walter Scott.

Here's a health to those we love best—
Our noble selves—God bless us;
None better and many a damn sight worse.
Drink today, and drown all sorrow;
You shall, perhaps, not do it tomorrow.
                    —Beaumont and Fletcher.

TO TOLERATION

Here's to the man of toleration,
Who shapes his views with moderation.
Theology and ignorance combined
Make bigotry, and that makes all men blind.
And streams of ruin from this common source
Have swept the world with devastating force.

With roasts and toasts the revelers cloy,
Their vitals, when 'round the board they sup,
And merrily chase the bubble Joy.
Which dances gaily in friendship's cup.
                              —Asa Arp.

He drank strong waters and his speech was coarse;
He purchased raiment and forbore to pay;
He stuck a trusting junior with a horse,
And won Gymkhanas in a doubtful way.
Then, 'twixt a vice and folly, turned aside
To do good deeds, and straight to cloak them, lied.
                    —Rudyard Kipling, "A Bank Fraud"

You may talk o' gin an' beer
When you're quartered safe out 'ere,
An' you're sent to penny-fights an' Aldershot it;
But if it comes to slaughter
You will do your work on water,
An' you'll lick the bloomin' boots of 'im that's got it.
                    —Rudyard Kipling, from "Gunga Din"

TOMMY

I went into a public-'ouse to get a pint o' beer,
The publican 'e up an' sez, "We serve no red-coats here."
The girls be'ind the bar they laughed an' giggled fit to die.
I outs into the street again, an' to myself sez I:
    O it's Tommy this, an' Tommy that, an' "Tommy go away";
    But it's "Thank you, Mister Atkins, 'when the band begins to play,
    The band begins to play, my boys, the band begins to play,
    O it's "Thank you, Mister Atkins," when the band begins to play.

I went into a theater as sober as could be,
They give a drunk civilian room, but 'adn't none for me;
They sent me to the gallery or round the music-'alls,
But when it comes to fightin', Lord! they'll shove me in the stalls.
    For it's Tommy this, an' Tommy that, an' "Tommy wait outside";
    But it's "Special train for Atkins," when the trooper's on the tide,
    The troopship's on the tide, my boys, etc.

O makin' mock o' uniforms that guard you while you sleep
Is cheaper than them uniforms, an' they're starvation cheap;
An' hustlin' drunken sodgers when they're goin' large a bit
Is five times better business than paradin' in full kit.
    Then it's Tommy this, an' Tommy that, an' "Tommy, 'ow's yer soul?"
    But it's "Thin red line of 'eroes" when the drums begin to roll,
    The drums begin to roll, my boys, etc.

We aren't no thin red 'eroes, nor we aren't no blackguards too,
But single men in barricks, most remarkable like you;
An' if sometimes our conduck isn't all your fancy paints,
Why, single men in barricks don't grow into plaster saints.
    While it's Tommy this, an' Tommy that, an' "Tommy fall be'ind;"
    But it's "Please to walk in front, sir," when there's trouble in the wind,
    There's trouble in the wind, my boys, etc.
          —Rudyard Kipling

Smoking

THE BETROTHED

"You must choose between me and your cigar"
Open the old cigar-box, get me a Cuba stout,
For things are running crossways, and Maggie and I are out.

We quarreled about Havanas—we fought o'er a good cheroot,
And I know she is exacting, and she says I am a brute.

Open the old cigar-box—let me consider a space;
In the soft blue veil of the vapor, musing on Maggie's face.

Maggie is pretty to look at—Maggie's a loving lass,
But the prettiest cheeks must wrinkle, the truest of loves must pass.

There's peace in a Laranaga, there's calm in a Henry Clay,
But the best cigar in an hour is finished and thrown away—

Thrown away for another as perfect and ripe and brown—
But I could not throw away Maggie for fear o' the talk o' the town!

Maggie, my wife at fifty—gray and dour and old—
With never another Maggie to purchase for love or gold!

And the light of Days that have Been, the dark of the Days that Are,
And Love's torch stinking stale, like the butt of a dead cigar—

The butt of a dead cigar you are bound to keep in your pocket—
With never a new one to light tho' it's charred and black to the socket.

Open the old cigar-box—let me consider a while—
Here is a mild Manilla—there is a wifely smile.

Which is the better portion—bondage bought with a ring,
Or a harem of dusky beauties, fifty tied in a string?

Counselors cunning and silent—comforters true and tried,
And never a one of the fifty to sneer at a rival bride.

Thought in the early morning, solace in time of woes,
Peace in the hush of the twilight, balm ere my eyelids close.

This will the fifty give me, asking naught in return,
With only a Suttee's passion—to do their duty and burn.

This will the fifty give me, when they are spent and dead,
Five times other fifties shall be my servants instead.

The furrows of far-off Java, the isles of the Spanish Main,
When they hear my harem is empty, will send me my brides again.

I will take no heed to their raiment, nor food for their mouths withal,
So long as the gulls are nesting, so long as the showers fall.

I will scent 'em with best vanilla, with tea will I temper their hides,
And the Moor and the Mormon shall envy who read of the tale of my brides.

For Maggie has written a letter to give me my choice between
The wee little whimpering Love and the great god Nick o' Teen.

And I have been servant of Love for barely a twelvemonth clear,
But I have been Priest of Partagas a matter of seven year;

And the gloom of my bachelor days is flecked with the cheery light
Of stumps that I burned to Friendship and Pleasure and Work and Fight.

And I turn my eyes to the future that Maggie and I must prove,
But the only light on the marshes is the Will-o'-the-Wisp of Love.

Will it see me safe through my journey, or leave me bogged in the mire?
Since a puff of tobacco can cloud it, shall I follow the fitful fire?

Open the old cigar-box—let me consider anew—
Old friends, and who is Maggie that I should abandon you?

A million surplus Maggies are willing to bear the yoke;
And a woman is only a woman, but a good cigar is a Smoke.

Light me another Cuba; I hold to my first-sworn vows
If Maggie will have no rival, I'll have no Maggie for spouse!

It's better to smoke her than in the hereafter.

TOAST TO THREE LOVED ONES

My gentle Lady Cigarette. who would not find you fair?
Your slender bit of loveliness of grace and beauty rare.
You dress in modest frock of white, but sure no guileless maiden
Could know the witcheries and lures with which your soul is laden,
Enwreathed with fragrant floating clouds you seem a spirit sent
From magic Eastern climes to charm men's souls to devilment,
And he who tastes the pleasant, strange seduction of your kiss
Would barter all his heart holds dear to keep that only bliss.

And you, my stately Dame Cigar, in sober brown arrayed,
A goodly matron, worthier far than any heedless maid.
You lend contentment to my soul and fill my hours of rest
With calm and peaceful reveries, and dreams serene and blest.
With you, good lady, I am not the slave of any man;
The equal of them all I sit and smoke and hope and plan
For all the solid comfort you have given, and still give,
Accept my loyalty, good dame, so long as I shall live.

And now my pipe, first love and last, my sweetheart old and true,
I give my meed of fullest praise to you and only you.
Companion of my wanderings through fair and stormy weather,
We've shared the ups and downs of life in harmony together.
Your smoke has mixed with smoke of friends we'll never see again,
You've cheered me as we sat night long to wield my foolish pen.
You've made good luck seem better, you have dulled misfortune's stroke,
My dear old Pipe! Ah, here's a light! It's time to have a smoke.

TO CONTENTMENT

Oh, there is not in life a pleasure so sweet
As to sit near the window and tilt up your feet,
To puff a Havana whose flavor just suits,
And gaze at the world through the toes of your boots.

Death

Death's but a path that must be trod
If man would ever pass to God.
                    —Parnell.

Weep not for him who dieth,
For he sleeps and is at rest,
And the couch whereon he lieth
Is the green earth's quiet breast
                         —Mrs. Norton.

To die—to sleep—
No more, and by a sleep to say we end
The heartache, and the thousand natural shocks
That flesh is heir to; 'tis a consummation
Devoutly to be wished.
                    —Shakespeare.

When musing on companions gone
We double feel ourselves alone.
    —Scott.

     ❧

Strange, is it not? that of the myriads who
Before us passed the door of darkness through,
Not one returns to tell us of the road,
Which to discover we must travel too.

     ❧

Through the street of By-and-by, journeying forever,
Slowly one comes at last to the house of Never.

     ❧

TOAST TO DEATH

If I should die tonight
And you should come to my cold corpse and say,
Weeping and heartsick o'er my lifeless clay—
If I should die. tonight
And you should come in deepest grief and woe—
And say: "Here's that ten dollars that I owe,"
I might rise in my large cravat
And say, "What's that?"

If I should die tonight
And you should come to my cold corpse and kneel,
Clasping my bier to show the grief you feel,
I say, if I should die tonight
And you should come to me, and there and then
Just even hint 'bout paying me that ten,
I might arise the while,
But I'd drop dead again.
                              —Ben King.

If you see my tombstone,
Don't pass it by,
Please piss on my grave,
'Cause I'll always be dry.

If down here I chance to die,
    Solemnly I beg you take
All that is left of "I"
    To the Hills for old sake's sake.
Pack me very thoroughly
    In the ice that used to slake
Pegs I drank when I was dry—
    This observe for old sake's sake.
                        —Rudyard Kipling, from
                        "A Ballad of Burial"

THE EXPLANATION

Love and Death once ceased their strife
At the Tavern of Man's Life.
Called for wine, and threw—alas!—
Each his quiver on the grass.
When the bout was o'er they found
Mingled arrows strewed the ground.
Hastily they gathered then
Each the loves and lives of men.
Ah, the fateful dawn deceived!
Mingled arrows each one sheaved:
Death's dread armory was stored
With the shafts he most abhorred:
Love's light quiver groaned beneath
Venom-headed darts of Death.

Thus it was they wrought our woe
At the Tavern long ago.
Tell me, do our masters know,
Loosing blindly as they fly,
Old men love while young men die?
— Rudyard Kipling

Patriotism

OUR COUNTRY'S EMBLEM

The Lily of France may fade,
  The Thistle and Shamrock wither,
The oak of England may decay,
  But the Stars shine on forever.

⚬

Here's to the American Eagle: The liberty
  bird that permits no liberties.

⚬

Our National Birds,
  THE AMERICAN EAGLE,
  THE THANKSGIVING TURKEY.
May one give us peace in all our states,
The other a piece for all our plates.

Come fill the glass and drain the bowl;
May Love and Bacchus still agree;
And every American warm his soul
With Cupid, wine and Liberty.

⚬

May the blossoms of liberty never be
  blighted.

⚬

May the tree of liberty flourish around
  the globe and may every human
  being partake of its fruits.

May the prison gloom be cheered by the rays of hope, and liberty fetter the arms of oppression.

⚘

May all mankind make free to enjoy the blessings of liberty; but never take the liberty to subvert the principles of freedom.

⚘

TO OUR DEPARTED COMRADES

To those we loved, the loveliest and the best
That from his vintage rolling Time has pres't;
Who drank their cup many a round of yore,
And one by one crept silently to rest.
—Persian Verse.

Here's to our President—May he always merit the esteem and affection of a people, ever ready to bestow gratitude on those who deserve it.

⚘

THE FLAG

When freedom from her mountain height
Unfurled her standard to the air,
She tore the azure robe of night,
And set the stars of glory there.
She mingled with its gorgeous dyes
The milky baldric of the skies,
And striped its pure, celestial white
With streakings of the morning light.
                    —Joseph Rodman Drake.

Here's to American valor,
May no war require it, but may it ever be
    ready for every foe.

TO THE PRESIDENT

Here's to the President—His
    rights and no more.

Here's to our Chief
    Magistrate—May the greet-
    ing which he has received
    from the hearts of the people
    be repaid by his faithful
    honor and fidelity.

TO OUR ARMY AND NAVY

Success to our army, success to our fleet,
May our foes be compelled to bow down at our feet.

TO WAR

War begets Poverty—Poverty, Peace—
Peace begets Riches—Fate will not cease—
Riches beget Pride—Pride is War's ground—
War begets Poverty—and so the world goes round.

Here's to commerce universally extended,
And blood-stained war forever ended.

May the sword of liberty smite the despots who combine
  against the freedom of our race.

May Columbia's brave defenders
Ever stand for the good of her cause;
While such we can toast them, no rogues or pretenders,
Can injure our dear Constitution or laws.

Here's to all those who have fought and bled for America.

TOAST TO THE SOLDIER

Great telescopes have reveal'd the spots on the sun,
And dissolv'd nebulae into constellations;
But 'tis the silent man behind the gun,
Who shapes the destiny of all nations.
                    —Asa Arp.

The U stands for the Union eternal,
The S for the Stripes and Stars,
The A for our Army undefeated,
The victor in a dozen wars;

The U stands for our "Uncle Sammy."
The S for our Ships in stern array,
The A for the Almighty One who guards us—
That's the meaning of U. S. A.

Here's to America—And
may the land of our
nativity be ever the abode
of freedom, and the
birthplace of heroes.